Exp

Everyone can coach throwing

or teach themselves to throw,

using the mechanics and drills

I have described in this book.

Just follow my training philosophy:

Training Philosophy

Do each repetition **right**.....
do each repetition with **intensity**....
or.....
do each repetition **again**.

Coach Bill Renner

Coaching Note

My coaching phrases are highlighted in yellow. Use these when coaching the mechanics. They will create the mental thoughts and visual needed to throw well. They will also give you the vocabulary to communicate "fixes" as you train.

A recommended training program to teach these throwing specific mechanics is at the end of this book. Do all the repetitions and you will build the arm strength and body movement synchronization to be a very accurate passer. And, remember to *watch the ball flight on each throw for feedback on what mechanic needs to be fixed for the next repetition to be perfect!*

"The ball flies <u>exactly</u> where your body mechanics make it fly. It does not randomly go where it wants."

Coach Bill Renner

Drill Sequencing
For Skill Perfection and Correction

This throwing drill sequence builds on itself. Do the first drill right because it is part of the next drill also.

Thus, you must strive to master the mechanics of the first drill to do the next drill successfully.

The benefit of such a sequence is that any throwing technique error you make can be traced back to one of these drills.

Then, you can go back and do that specific drill to fix your throwing technique.

This gives you the ability to control how good you become. Because,

"if you can do the <u>drill</u>, you can do the <u>skill</u>."

Coach Bill Renner

Release Drill
Quarterback Throwing Mechanics Drill 1

Purpose: to develop spotting a target with the eyes
to develop the coil of the upper body
to develop the front arm tuck
to develop the wrist/finger release position
to develop the proper ball release point

Release Drill Setup
Stand 10 yards apart from a throwing partner. Stand with your two toes on a line with your knees, hips and shoulders squarely <u>facing</u> your partner. Keep your feet stationary and facing your partner as you throw. Do not move them. Rotate only your upper body to throw. NO stride.

Stance
Hold the football with two hands in the drop back position, *"chest to chin height"*, no higher and no lower. The end of the ball is pointed at a 45 degree angle to the ground insuring that your *wrist* is *"loaded"*, or cocked, to release at the right moment. Stand tall and bend your knees so you are in athletic position with your shoulders over your knees and your knees over your toes. Focus your eyes on your throwing target, your

partner's face.

Throwing at a Target
I believe that you don't have to ask a quarterback what he saw or where he was looking after a throw because:

You <u>always throw</u> where you are looking,
and you <u>always hit</u> what you are looking at.

Consequently where you look during this throwing progression is extremely important.

Training Accuracy

During all these drills, the eyes need to focus on the face of the receiver or partner. He needs to have "*laser eyes*". His "*throwing target*" for all throws will be the "*face of his partner*". His "*throwing miss area*" is shoulder tip to shoulder tip width and no lower than chest height. Any throw outside of this defined area is a mistake and a wasted repetition.

If you don't give the quarterback specific accuracy parameters
for every throw including any warm-ups,
then you will not develop his accuracy to the maximum level,
or, to a level you will be content with on game day.

Target Accuracy Error Feedback

Use the feedback of where the miss occurred to correct the mechanic mistake for the next throw. This is a most critical component of this program. When you are correcting each throw for accuracy and fixing it on the next rep you are doing "*deep practice*".

Deep practice means you monitor each repetition for a mistake, you know when you make an error and you know how to fix it. The ability to deep practice is extremely important if you want to become elite or to be able to reach your full potential.

Here are the general target error rules for a quarterback for all these drills:

> Missing High – ball is released too early
> Missing Low – ball is released too late

Any miss left or right of the target indicates that the throwing arm path started outside the vertical line to the target. In other words, the throwing arm came across the body to throw the ball. This is caused by:

> *front arm movement and tuck that rotates around the body and pulls the throwing arm on a circular path to the target instead of a linear or straight path to the target*

So, when a throw is to the left or right of the face (target) of the throwing partner then the arm was not on a perfect linear path to the target. <u>Focus on keeping the front arm stable and pointed at the target. Move your chest toward the front arm as you throw</u>.

To summarize:

> <u>Missing Left of Target</u> – arm path not toward target;
> ball is released too late

> <u>Missing Right of Target</u> – arm path not toward target;
> ball is release too early

Coil and Rotation of the Upper Body

To start the coiling of the upper body, "*push the ball backward*" with the front hand. It is the left hand for a right handed quarterback. This helps load the upper body coil quicker and with more energy.

It is natural to feel like you can't rotate or coil as much as you like. Keeping the hips square to the target inhibits hip rotation and causes this feeling. We want to isolate the upper body and develop the oblique muscles, side muscles, to pull aggressively through the delivery and release motion and this is the method to do that.

Rotate or coil your upper body to the point where your "*front shoulder* is almost *pointing straight at your target*". It will stall out about 10-15 degrees short of that but this mind set will get you to maximum rotation. Keep your upper body tall as you do this. Don't lean backward.

Notice:

- ➢ Feet stable and toes straight ahead
- ➢ Hips rotated
- ➢ Ball pushed back with front hand
- ➢ Eyes like lasers on target
- ➢ Upper body tall

6

Starting the Arm Forward

Start the uncoiling of the upper body and the moving of the arm to throw by taking your front hand off the ball and tucking the elbow of your *"front arm downward and tight to your chest"*. Move the chest to the arm and not the other way around. Keep the front arm stationary.

Getting the Ball On the Target Line

To get the ball on line to the target the *"throwing elbow* needs to come through *above the shoulder line"*. As you tuck your front elbow you will notice a slight shoulder tilt, left to right, that will cause the throwing elbow to be elevated to this position.

Keep the throwing elbow above the shoulder line throughout the throwing motion.
Dropping the elbow below the shoulder line causes the arm to cut across the body or rotate away from the target.

The throwing elbow will be up and out at a 45 degree angle with the hand inside the elbow. As the arm comes through, think about *"pointing your index and middle fingers directly at your target "*.

Your "laser eyes" are telling your fingers where to point.

"Hold your upper body perfectly stable" while the arm is moving to the target. Any movement of the upper body forward, backward, left or right will change the arm path to the target and create an inability to control the flight path of the ball.

Upper body movement during the arm movement to throw causes inconsistent arm paths which causes inconsistent accuracy.

Releasing the Ball

The ball is released just in *"front of the face"* at the point where the triceps or arm is almost fully extended. This is the point where:

- your hips have fully uncoiled
- your belly button is facing your target
- your arm is at maximum speed
- your triceps muscle is fully contracted
- your weight has shifted to your toes
- your upper body is upright and stable

Now your whole body is behind the throw, the ball is on the target line and <u>you can control the flight of the ball</u>.

Any deviation from these essential elements of the release will cause an errant throw.

Finger Tip Release

The fingers are spread out on the football with fingertip pressure applied as you hold it. You should hold the ball firmly but not with a "death grip". As you release the ball it will roll off the fingers smoothly and easily with the middle and index finger being the last two to release off the ball.

Remember that these are the two fingers point at your target so a smooth roll of the ball off these fingers provides the spin that keeps the ball on line to the target.

Wrist Action

The wrist which was in the "loaded position" during the drop back phase is now ready to snap and accelerate the fingers off the ball to provide greater spin to the ball. As you feel the middle and index finger leaving the ball, snap your wrist to accelerate these fingers. This "*wrist snap*" will cause your hand to rotate inward so your pinky finger is facing upward and your thumb is facing downward.

This wrist snap is a timing element that you develop a feel for. And, this is why you will do this throwing sequence every time as a warm-up before you throw to moving targets.

*Sequencing and timing movements
need to be practiced and "warmed up"
BEFORE you are asked to perform or do skills,
like throwing at moving targets.*

Finishing the Throw

*Decelerating the arm improperly is what
causes most arm injuries.*

The arm must continue to move forward at the same rate of speed just after release. It gradually decelerate through the finish until it reaches the opposite hip. This insures that your arm is "*accelerating through the throw*" and has ample time to reduce speed or decelerate without causing damage to the arm over time.

"*Arm speed at and through the release*" is also paramount to keeping the ball on line to the target.

*The faster the arm is at release
the longer distances the quarterback
is able to throw the ball "on a line".*

*Arm speed equals ball flight distance
and "on a line" throws.*

Continue the upper body rotation after the release so that the back part of the throwing shoulder is pointing at the target. This demonstrates that the arm was "*accelerating to and through*" the release point.

9

Coaching Notes

You must learn to release the ball from the <u>same point in front of your body</u> every time in order to be accurate.

You can have a different arm angle for the release but the same release point must be reached in order to have the same arm velocity and accuracy on every throw.

An <u>early release point</u> results in high passes with poor accuracy. A <u>late release</u> results in low passes with reduced velocity and accuracy.

Repetition Sequence

Do these 15 throws for this <u>Release Drill</u>. The distances are how far apart you are from your partner.

10 yards – 5 throws
15 yards – 5 throws
20 yards – 5 throws

Release Drill Execution Goal

Do it **RIGHT**.....

focus on accuracy; aim at your partner's face <u>*every time*</u>.

Do it with **INTENSITY**.....

*keep track of how many times you hit his face
from each distance; a total of 15 points
<u>i.e.</u> 14 out of 15*

Do it **AGAIN**....

*Record your results for each distance
and for an overall accuracy percentage
For example:*

*10 yards = 5 out of 5
15 yards = 3 out of 5
20 yards = 4 out of 5
Total = 12 out of 15*

Work toward a perfect score, 15 out of 15.

10

Rotation-Weight Transfer Drill
Quarterback Throwing Mechanics Drill 2

Purpose: to develop the width of the throwing stance
to develop the proper front foot movement
to develop the <u>shifting of weight</u> from the
back foot to the front foot
to develop upper body stability in weight transfer
to develop a feel for the SHORT STEP throw

Rotation-Weight Transfer Drill Setup
Stand 10 yards apart and perpendicular
to a throwing partner. Your <u>shoulders are
slightly open</u> so that <u>your chin and eyes</u>
are <u>pointing directly at your target</u>, not
your front shoulder. The position of your
front shoulder affects your peripheral
vision.

*If you close your front shoulder, point it to
your throwing partner, you restrict your
peripheral vision to your left.*

Your <u>feet</u> need to be <u>wider than your
shoulders</u> to provide you with <u>a balanced
platform</u> to throw from.

*At times in the pocket you may not be
able to step to throw. You must make "no
step throws". This "wide base" will enable you to rotate your
hips for a powerful throw.*

Stance
Align your body in *"athletic position"*; upper body is tall with
shoulders over the knees and knees bent over the toes. Your
weight is evenly distributed on the balls of both feet. You
should feel like you are in <u>a position to be able to bounce on
your toes</u>.

Your <u>front foot is off-set to the left of your target</u> so that your front shoulder points slightly to the left of your target.

If you point your front foot at your target then your shoulders will be "closed off" to your target or pointing to the right of your target.

Hold the football with two hands in the drop back position, *"chest to chin height"*, no lower and no higher. The end of the ball is pointed at a 45 degree angle to the ground insuring that your *wrist* is *"loaded"*, or cocked, to release at the right moment. Focus your eyes like lasers, *"laser eyes"*, on your partners face. Remember,

You <u>always throw</u> where you are looking,
and you <u>always hit</u> what you are looking at.

Shifting the Weight

To start the transfer of weight to the back foot, *"push the ball backward"* with the front hand. It is the left hand for a right handed quarterback. <u>At the same time shift the weight to the instep of your back foot</u>.

This is a <u>shifting</u> of the weight <u>not</u> a <u>tilting</u> of the upper body backward.

As your weight shifts, lift the heel of your front foot off the ground so only your toe is touching. This will put 80% of your weight on your back foot. This is necessary to *"load your back foot"* for a forceful push and transfer of energy from the lower body to the throw.

You must avoid "tilting the upper body".
The upper body must stay "tall holding the ball" and <u>stable</u>, not moving left or right or forward or backward, as you shift your weight.

Tilting the body backward to shift the weight will cause the weight to be on the outside of the back foot.

This does not allow you to make a quick and powerful push to initiate the throw. It causes you to have a slow release.

12

The final weight loading on the back foot occurs when the ball moves backward outside the body with the front foot starting to rotate forward so <u>the toe points at but to the left of the target</u>.

Notice: ━━━━━━━━━━━━━━━━━━━━▶
- ➢ Upper body tall and stable, no tilt
- ➢ Front foot off the target line
- ➢ Back foot loaded and ready to push
- ➢ Ball outside the body in fully loaded position
- ➢ Eyes like lasers on target
- ➢ Upper body tall

You do not step directly at your target to throw. This puts your front foot in the way of your hips rotating all the way to the target.

Your <u>front foot steps slightly to the left of the target</u> off of the direct line of your target.

This allows your hips to fully rotate square to the target with maximum velocity at ball release.

Starting the Movement Forward
Push off the instep of your back foot to start the movement forward. Do not tilt your upper body forward to start the movement. Keep your upper body stable as you push.

As you start to push, your front foot lands and provides a stable base for your hips and upper body to uncoil around. The width of your step needs to be wider than your shoulders.

Arm Position
Before the arm starts forward:

- The <u>elbow should be in a 90 degree angle with the upper arm parallel to the ground</u>.
- The <u>shoulders</u> are <u>parallel to the ground</u>.
- The <u>front arm</u> is out <u>in front of the body</u> tucked and ready for the upper body to move toward it.

This front arm position enables you to hold the hip-shoulder separation as long as possible to create the maximum uncoiling speed for maximum arm speed.

Hip and Shoulder Separation for Arm Speed
Your front foot is open with knee pointing forward. Your shoulders are still perpendicular to the target creating the *"upper body coil"* that will provide the rotational force that gives your arm speed.

The degree of "upper body coil" or twisting separation between the hips and shoulders is what determines arm speed.

The greater the separation between the hips and shoulders, the more arm speed your body can generate.

Release Drill Takes Over
At the point where your front foot is in position and your upper body is coiled to start the throw, you are now in the <u>Release Drill technique area</u>.

If you focused on the <u>Release Drill techniques</u> in the previous drill you can now automatically or subconsciously finish the throw.

Remember to:

✓ Keep your "laser eyes" locked in on the target
✓ Keep your upper body stable
✓ Aggressively rotate your hips
✓ Feel the smooth release of the ball off your finger tips
✓ And, *"accelerate through the throw"*

14

Coaching Note

Learning the correct upper body movement during the Rotation-Weight Transfer Drill teaches the arm to remain online with the target.

The <u>throwing arm</u> does not come around the body in a rotational arc. It <u>starts at the target</u> and <u>remains online to the target throughout the motion</u>.

This is <u>one key technique</u> that enables you <u>to control ball flight</u> and <u>become an accurate passer</u>.

Repetition Sequence

Do these 15 throws for this <u>Rotation-Weight Tansfer Drill</u>. The distances are how far apart you are from your partner.

10 yards – 5 throws
15 yards – 5 throws
20 yards – 5 throws

Rotation-Weight Transfer Drill Execution Goal

Do it **RIGHT**.....

focus on accuracy; *aim at your partner's face <u>every time</u>.*

Do it with **INTENSITY**.....

keep track of how many times you hit his face
from each distance; a total of 15 points
<u>i.e.</u> 14 out of 15

Do it **AGAIN**....

Record your results for each distance
and for an overall accuracy percentage
For example:

10 yards = 5 out of 5
15 yards = 3 out of 5
20 yards = 4 out of 5
Total = 12 out of 15

Work toward a perfect score, 15 out of 15.

Crossover Balance Drill
Quarterback Throwing Mechanics Drill 3

Purpose: to develop upper body stability in drop movement
to develop crossover foot movement dropping back
to develop change of direction from dropping
back to moving into throwing position

Crossover Balance Drill Setup
Stand 10 yards apart and perpendicular to a throwing partner. Your <u>shoulders are slightly open</u> so that <u>your chin and eyes</u> are <u>pointing directly at your target</u>, not your front shoulder.

The position of your front shoulder affects your peripheral vision.

If you close your front shoulder, point it to your throwing partner, you restrict your peripheral vision to your left.

Your <u>feet</u> need to be <u>wider than your shoulders</u> to provide you with <u>a balanced platform</u> to throw from.

Crossover Step
Take a 6-8 inch *"crossover step"* with your front foot to begin the movement backward. The movement backward <u>is not</u> initiated with the upper body tilting backward.

The upper body needs to remain upright and stable and with the shoulders slightly open, as in your pre-movement alignment, as you crossover step backward.

16

<u>There is no compromise in this upper body stability technique</u>.

A quarterback that uses <u>upper body sway</u> to move backward and then forward will have <u>inconsistent accuracy</u>, the <u>result of inconsistent weight transfer.</u>

This inconsistency ultimately produces inconsistent release points of the football; release points that are too early or too late and demonstrated by passes that are too high or too low.

Can upper body sway be mastered to the point which that person can be an effective quarterback passer?

Yes. Any technique can be honed to be effective even if it is less than what is desired. However, when stressful situations are applied to less than perfect technique, those technique errors are magnified and cannot be overcome with sheer determination.

In other words, do you want to be "*effective*" or "*elite*".

Elite players perform in stressful or pressure situations because their techniques allow them to play and think at high speeds when the game and situations demand it.

Train to be ELITE not EFFECTIVE!
Do the right techniques.

Balance Step

Once the crossover step <u>hits the ground</u>, the other foot is lifted off the ground, reaches back and is <u>planted outside shoulder width</u> to establish the wide stable base for throwing.

Do not pick the back foot up off the ground until the crossover step has touched the ground.

A quarterback always wants to have one foot on the ground at all times to be able to initiate a throw at any time.

The <u>weight</u> should be <u>balanced</u> and maintained on the "*<u>inside of the foot</u>*" not rolling to the outside part of the foot. With 85% of the weight on the ball of the foot and 15% distributed along the arch and heel of the foot.

You should be able to pick up your heel without disturbing your balance when you are in the proper "balance foot position".

From this position, you can make an aggressive, forceful push to move forward.

When the weight is on the outside edge of the foot, you will first have to transfer the weight to the inside of the foot to be able to push forward which necessitates more time to get to the throwing position and results in a slower release.

Good "*balance plant step*" position

> Weight on instep
> Upper body stable
> Ball in throwing ready position

<u>Balance Step to Rotation-Weight Transfer Position</u>

Once the balance step has been planted in the ground, transfer the weight so that the <u>hips sink</u> and <u>the knee bends</u> to "*load*" the thigh and hips for a forceful push forward. This also creates the "*balanced athletic stance*" you need in the pocket.

"*Standing tall in the pocket*" <u>does not mean taking the athletic bend out of your knees</u> which most people interpret that to mean. It <u>means keeping your **upper body tall**</u> while your lower body is in an athletic position.

When you are in this "*balanced athletic position*", you are now simply going to perform the <u>Rotation-Weight Transfer Drill</u> and then the <u>Release Drill techniques.</u>

Rotation Weight Transfer Drill   **Release Drill**

This picture sequence demonstrates the importance of mastering each drill in this sequence as you progress to be a good thrower.

Coaching Note

The proper body balance and control during the crossover balance step will allow all the energy to be stored in the hips and thighs for a powerful rotation of the hips when the throwing motion is initiated.

Swaying the body forward and backward to crossover and plant forces the body to expend energy to rebalance itself to make the throw and not accumulate the power from the foot movement to transfer to the hips.

Repetition Sequence

Do these 15 throws for this <u>Crossover Balance Drill</u>. The distances are how far apart you are from your partner.

10 yards – 5 throws
15 yards – 5 throws
20 yards – 5 throws

Crossover Balance Drill Execution Goal

Do it **RIGHT**…..

focus on accuracy; aim at your partner's face <u>every time</u>.

Do it with **INTENSITY**…..

*keep track of how many times you hit his face
from each distance; a total of 15 points
i.e. 14 out of 15*

Do it **AGAIN**….

*Record your results for each distance
and for an overall accuracy percentage
For example:*

*10 yards = 5 out of 5
15 yards = 3 out of 5
20 yards = 4 out of 5
Total = 12 out of 15*

Work toward a perfect score, 15 out of 15.

Crossover Balance Hitch Step Drill
Quarterback Throwing Mechanics Drill 4

Purpose: to develop footwork for deeper pattern throws
        to develop upper body stability during forward
           pocket movement
        to develop a timing feel for longer throws

Crossover Balance Hitch Step Drill Setup

Stand 10 yards apart and perpendicular to a throwing partner. Your <u>shoulders are slightly open</u> so that <u>your chin and eyes</u> are <u>pointing directly at your target</u>, not your front shoulder.

The position of your front shoulder affects your peripheral vision.

If you close your front shoulder, point it to your throwing partner, you restrict your peripheral vision to your left.

Your <u>feet</u> need to be <u>wider than your shoulders</u> to provide you with <u>a balanced platform</u> to throw from.

Crossover and Balance Step
The crossover and balance step are done the exact same way as described in the <u>Crossover Balance Drill</u> section.

This is the importance of the sequencing of the drills. They build on each other. If you do the first one right then you can focus on the next technique added to it while still building efficiency on the previous drill's technique.

Drill Sequence
1 - Release Drill------→ 2 - Rotation Weight Transfer Drill-------→
3 - Crossover Balance Drill--→4 -Crossover Balance Hitch Step Drill

Hitch Step Purpose
The hitch step is used in timing the quarterbacks drop steps with longer routes the receiver is running. i.e. post, corner, fade, comeback, dig, etc.

If you match the quarterbacks' steps with the receiver routes then the quarterback can use his footwork as a timing measure of when the ball needs to be released.

This is a Bill Walsh principle that I have found to be very effective in helping coaching quarterbacks. It gives them a physical timing tool to know when they should expect to release the ball to throw the route.

My phrase is:

"Your feet tell you when and your eyes tell you where."

I coach this principle during this drill so I can reinforce it when skills and team time are practiced.

Feet and Eyes Work Separate During the Hitch Step
It is important during this drill to train the eyes as well as the footwork.

The feet are working while the eyes are taking in the information to tell the quarterback if he can throw when his feet tell him to.

Make sure the eyes are looking at the target like" *lasers*" and the quarterback hits his triangle target of head to shoulder tips.

This is where game accuracy can be developed; the feet are moving but the eyes and mind are focused on the action down field.

Hitch Step and Upper Body Stability
The upper body remains upright and stable during the crossover, balance and hitch steps. Any movement or tilting, left, right, forward or backward, will disrupt the vision of the quarterback and the timing and release point of the ball.

Make sure the shoulders are tall, slightly open and the ball remains at the chest level during this entire crossover, balance and hitch step sequence. Movement comes from the waist down not from the upper body swaying or rotating/wobbly shoulders or rocking the ball shoulder to shoulder on the way back.

Hitch Step Mechanics
When you hit your back foot, *"balance step"*, you will not have all the weight on the back foot like it is during the *"no hitch"* or crossover balance drill.

In the crossover balance drill the goal is to hit the back foot and get the ball out as quickly as possible because the receiver is running a shorter route. i.e. slant, out, hitch, etc. Thus, when the foot hits the ground there it needs to be loaded up and ready to push to get the hips rotating to get the ball out of the quarterback's hand.

In a hitch step delivery, the weight will be balanced and more on the toes so that the quarterback can *"bounce up"* into the throw. 60% of weight on the back foot and 40% weight on the front foot but on the toes so that you can "hitch" step into the throw.

The back foot must still stop the backward movement
so it has more of the weight distribution
but it stops the backward movement without as much force
into the ground because the quarterback is not releasing the
ball as soon as the back foot hits the ground.

Hitch Step Feet Separation
In the hitch step, the <u>back foot</u> should <u>never touch the front foot</u> or get close enough so that the feet land less than shoulder width apart. If the feet land closer than shoulder width the quarterback is off-balance with an unstable base to be able to throw the ball.

Remember, we want a "*wide stable base*" to deliver the ball which is what we practiced in Release and Rotation Weight transfer drill.

The feet bounce up, the back foot closes the distance to the front foot slightly, 4"-6" inches, but the <u>feet remain separated</u> and shoulder width or slightly less.

➡️

Whenever the feet get closer than shoulder width you have lost the stable "athletic base".

When the width of the feet or base becomes too narrow during the hitch step, the front has to take too long of a step to rewiden the base. This causes inconsistency in the timing of releasing the ball because of the extra time it takes to rewiden the base.

Hitch Step Base Sequence
The back foot will hit the ground first after the hitch movement is made to reestablish a base foot to push off and throw from. While this is happening the front foot is off the ground ready to land and begin delivery of the throw.

<u>It is important to "hitch step" as quickly as possible</u>. It is not a passive action. It is a willful, forceful push or bounce off both feet to reestablish a throwing base as quickly as possible to deliver the ball on time and on target.

With the back foot on the ground and front foot this movement now becomes the <u>Crossover Balance drill.</u>

Coaching Note
The hitch step allows you to generate more <u>body speed</u> which when accompanied with <u>upper body balance</u> and <u>body mechanics efficiency</u> will translate to additional arm speed. This speed is needed to make the longer distance throws in the 20 yard plus range for college or pro quarterbacks or the 15 plus yard range for the high school quarterback. The <u>hitch step</u> is also used as a <u>timing mechanism</u> on <u>long developing routes</u> such as the comeback, post, and corner.

Repetition Sequence
Do these 15 throws for this <u>Crossover Balance Hitch Step Drill</u>. The distances are how far apart you are from your partner.

10 yards – 5 throws
15 yards – 5 throws
20 yards – 5 throws

Crossover Balance Hitch Step Drill Execution Goal

Do it **RIGHT**…..

   focus on accuracy; *aim at your partner's face every time.*

Do it with **INTENSITY**…..

   keep track of how many times you hit his face
   from each distance; a total of 15 points
   i.e. 14 out of 15

Do it **AGAIN**….

   Record your results for each distance
   and for an overall accuracy percentage
   For example:

   10 yards = 5 out of 5
   15 yards = 3 out of 5
   20 yards = 4 out of 5
   Total = 12 out of 15

Work toward a perfect score, 15 out of 15.

Long Toss Drill
Quarterback Throwing Mechanics Drill 5

Purpose: to develop body position for deep ball throws
to develop footwork for late deep ball throws
to develop a timing feel for longer throws
to develop the ball flight arc for long TD throws

Long Toss Drill Setup
Stand <u>35 yards apart</u> and perpendicular to a throwing partner, preferably <u>on a line that runs from you to him</u>. If you are on a football field stand on a side line and throw across the field to your partner on the other hash mark. That distance is 35 yards.

Your <u>shoulders are slightly open</u> so that <u>your chin and eyes</u> are <u>pointing directly at your target</u>, not your front shoulder.

The position of your front shoulder affects your peripheral vision.

If you close your front shoulder, point it to your throwing partner, you restrict your peripheral vision to your left.

Your <u>feet</u> need to be <u>wider than your shoulders</u> to provide you with <u>a balanced platform</u> to throw from.

Long Toss Stance
Take a stance you would be in when you finished your drop and have set up to throw:

- <u>feet</u> slightly wider than shoulders (wide base)
- <u>body</u> is upright and balanced with weight on balls of feet
- <u>back foot</u> is on the line and <u>front foot</u> is to the left of the line
- <u>front shoulder</u> is tucked but angled open
- <u>chin, eyes and face</u> are right over the line pointing at the target

26

Long Toss Mechanics

- ➤ <u>Bounce</u> on your toes developing a rhythm
- ➤ <u>Rotate</u> your shoulders
- ➤ <u>Tilt the shoulders</u> slightly backward to create a higher launch angle for the release of the ball; this also loads your weight on your back foot
- ➤ Take a <u>short quick step</u> to start the throw
- ➤ Throw using only the uncoiling of your shoulders to generate energy.
- ➤ Use a <u>high and full release</u> which elongates the triceps muscle
- ➤ Release the ball with an <u>arc on the throw</u> so that the <u>ball falls directly on top of the head of your partner</u>
- ➤ Focus on the <u>ball traveling over top of the line</u> all the way to your partner

Long Toss Game Situation

The practical game situation for long toss drill is when:

- ✓ the quarterback has gone through all his short routes on a play
- ✓ the last option is the deep throw
- ✓ the rush is about in his face so hitching up or stepping up is not an option
- ✓ this situation generally occurs at the +40 yard line going in which is why the quarterback and his partner are 35 yards apart.

Ball Flight Arc Importance

When you are at the +40 yard line going in to score, the ball flight arc changes when you throw deep. The <u>ball</u> needs to have <u>arc</u> so that the <u>nose is coming downward as it descends</u>, a "*chimney throw*". This means to throw it like it could go down a chimney shaft on a roof, nose down.

This nose descending arc allows the receiver to be very accurate in judging where the ball is coming down.

He can go to that spot and make a good play on the ball.

Increasing the receiver judgment, increases the touchdown reception chances which is the goal when you reach the +40 going in area.

Long Toss Bounce

Long Toss Shoulder Tilt and Back Leg Load

High Full Release

High Ball Arc Flight

28

Coaching Note

Long toss will strengthen the arm and develop the proper body position for making the long throws.

When long throws are necessary, body position and release mechanics often become sacrificed for additional body energy exertion, they "try harder to throw it farther".

Long toss will develop the proper long throwing mechanics and convince them mentally that "*trying harder is not conducive to throwing farther*."

Repetition Sequence

Do these 10 throws for this Long Toss Drill.

35 yards apart – 10 throws

Long Toss Drill Execution Goal

Do it **RIGHT**.....

focus on accuracy; aim at the top of your partner's head every time.

Do it with **INTENSITY**.....

keep track of how many times you can land the ball so that the nose turns over and comes down on top of his head

i.e. 8 out of 10

Do it **AGAIN**....

Record your results for an overall accuracy percentage

For example:

35 yards = 7 out of 10

Work toward a perfect score, 10 out of 10.

Training Guidelines
For Throwing Progression Drills

Beginning Program Protocol

Duration: 3 weeks

Frequency: every other day – 3 days a week
Monday, Wednesday, Friday

Drill	Sets	Throws	Distances
Release	1	5 each	10, 15, 20
Rotation Weight Transfer	1	5 each	10, 15, 20
Crossover Balance	1	5 each	10, 15, 20
Crossover Balance Hitch	1	5 each	10, 15, 20
Long Toss	1	10	35 yards

Maintenance Program Protocol

Duration: 4 weeks

Frequency: every day – 5 days a week
Monday through Friday

Drill	Sets	Throws	Distances
Release	1	5 each	10, 15, 20
Rotation Weight Transfer	1	5 each	10, 15, 20
Crossover Balance	1	5 each	10, 15, 20
Crossover Balance Hitch	1	5 each	10, 15, 20
Long Toss	1	10	35 yards

Use this 7 week program to build good mechanics and core strength for throwing accurately.

"This drill sequence will enable you to coach the quarterback to be an accurate passer.

Being an accurate passer is essential to insuring the other players on the offense are effective.

Focus on being an accurate passer."

Coach Bill Renner

For additional coaching
educational materials
by Coach Bill Renner
visit:

www.billrennerfootball.com

Made in the USA
Middletown, DE
08 March 2017